LOVE

From The Heart

Kevin Barton

Edited by: Wenly Fowler

Love from the heart / by Kevin Barton.—1st ed.

22 p. cm.

ISBN 13: 978-976-8231-88-8

1. Bahamian poetry. 2. Poets – Bahamas. 3. Poems.

PR9220.9.B37 L68 2020

811—dc23

Pre-press and printed by:
Media Enterprises Ltd.,
P.O. Box N-9240, 31 Shirley Park Avenue
Nassau, Bahamas
Tel: 242.325.8210 | Fax: 242.325.8065
info@bahamasmedia.com
http//www.bahamasmedia.com

Table of Contents

Foreword by Pastor Wenly Fowler

I found these artistic expressions of love to be eclectic in
form, content, perspective and style; at times I found myself
on the rocks of the shore thinking quirky; only to sudden-
ly be swept away by a rapturous wave of verbal brilliance.
Much of the sentiments speak with simplistic eloquence to
the importance of assuring your significant other, of their
captivating physical beauty and your unshakable love.
Intentional effort was given to stress the gamut of love from
visual infatuation, to 'til death do us part' devotion. Embed-
ded in these declarations of love are the deliberate sensitivity
and truth that if love is experienced and sustained, on has to
be honest, patient, attentive, communicative, loyal, forgiving
supportive and sufficiently present.
We are relational beings by God's sovereign design. There-
fore, we should relate purposefully, wisely, respectfully and
in a God honouring manner. Your hereby invited to delve
into these multifaceted expressions of love- you will simile,
scratch your head, reflect and hopefully ignite your own cre-
ativity in expressing or strengthening you love relationship.

Introduction

This collection of love poems speak to the heart of lovers and people who one day will fall in love. I believe that God has put this desire to love and be loved in all of our hearts, to love and to feel love.
Love is a beautiful thing when done right, especially God's way.
I put together this collection of love poems to reignite, or rekindle the flames of love in marriages and in relationships around the world.
So ponder these words and see how they speak to you. Most of all, I hope and pray that you would be tremendously blessed.
Special thanks to Wenly Fowler, Harold Johnson and Tiana Johnson.

Love From The Heart

Synopsis: Love From the Heart was the first poem I have
ever written and it was written because I was challenged
from a friend over thirty-five years ago. One day, a friend
named Nicolas brought a poem to me that he swore he had
written no matter how much I insisted that he didn't because
I knew Nick did not have a poetic bone in his body. I told
him that I would show him how to write a poem and bring it
to him in the morning. I was so intrigued and excited by the
idea of writing this poem, that immediately when I got home
I had begun writing a few lines. I presented it to Nicolas the
next day and he was impressed by my work. This began the
beginning of my love for writing poetry.
My love for poetry in general however, began with one of
my Religious Knowledge teachers, Dr. Rev. O. A. Pratt. He
was a firm disciplinarian who did not play around when it
came to our education. He was a real man who taught me
many poems and teared up my behind on several occasions
when I could not recite the poems he gave me to learn.
(People often ask me how I am able to recite so many of my
poems from memory - 'das how! Dr. Pratt gave me a real
appreciation for memorization in literature).
There are three poems that I grew to love from my time
studying with Dr. Pratt. Drink to Me Only With Thine Eyes
by Ben Jonson, In Flanders Fields by John McCrae and
Invictus by William Ernest Henley were their names. As
a tribute to the authors, I have included their poetry in the
pages to follow.
Dr. O. A. Pratt, I have a great depth of gratitude to you for
awakening the poet in me.

Love From The Heart

There is a feeling deep within when I am in your presence.
A feeling of love and devotion
Stronger than any potion,
In my heart, there is a notion
That this is love.
I can't express it because it's real,
And it's what I feel:
Your warm embrace,
Your smiling face,
Your gracious eyes
That hypnotize.
I have no fear
When you are near,
Because to me you are so dear.
I can't be wrong,
This feeling is strong.
This must be love.
Sooner or later you'll get to the root,
Sooner or later you'll know the truth:
I am in love.
At night, I have visions of you,
This feeling so deep
That I cannot sleep,
And at night I even weep:
This must be LOVE.

"Warning! Warning!! Warning!!!"

This book of love poems should not be taken for granted because the words contained in this book is meant for lovers, marriage and people who are seeking real relationships for life.

People's hearts are at stake here, so read carefully and prayerfully and then apply. The reward or consequence can, and will be a life-changing experience where hearts are joined or broken forever.

So heed the author's advice before using this powerful book of love poems.

"I Do, I Do"

I do, I do, you know it too
Girl please tell me what more I need to do

You are my heart and soul
You even play with my mind
But I am sure, you are a great find, we will be just fine

I need to know if we are on the right track,
Because my love, there is no turning back
Yours is the hands I want to hold
And I want to do so when we are old

Because I say it and you know it's true,
I do, I do and you know it too.

"Could Love Be Defined?"

Could love be defined,
With heart and mind?

Could love be displayed,
In a beautiful parade?

Could love last a lifetime
With songs, poems and rhythm and rhyme?
Could love bring happiness?

Could love be displayed,
In a beautiful parade?

Could love last a lifetime
With songs, poems and
Rhythm and rhyme

I want to know
Can love be defined?
It will take heart, soul body and mind

Can love be defined,
Because true love I want to find

"Love Me"

Love is the hope of many lonely hearts
Love is that emotion that move one to do and act on
behalf of others

How do I express this love to you
Can I tell you every day
That I love you?
Will you let me show this love,
With the tangible things in life?
Will these roses and carnations do,
Or must I say I love you too,
And can I call you on the phone,
To make all my feelings known?
Will our hearts be joined as one,
And will we have lots of fun?
I hope with the passing of time
Our love will grow and grow
And family and friends will come
To know, that this love is
For real!

"My Lover"

In my life you do all things right.
You fill my life with laughter
And you add color to everything
We do
You are my lover.

The day we met
There was something special about you,
And I know you were, for real!
Something, about you made me
Take another look
Who would have known that you would
Steal my heart,
And make me the happiest person in the world
I can't get enough of you!
Your body, mind and soul

You are my lover
I thank God for bringing you into my life
You are my lover!

"Keeping It Real"

You know how I feel,
Let's keep it real.

I told you time and time again,
You have the key to my heart
And my love for you will never die

It gets stronger and stronger
Every day
"So darling, don't play"

There is nothing I won't do for you,
And you know it's true.
"So darling, don't play"

I hope these words
Are truly heartfelt.
And I am keeping it real,
Cause you know how I feel.

"So darling it's because I'm keeping it real.

"Sorry"

Sorry for taking our love for granted
Sorry all because I did not understand it

Sorry for my selfish act
Because there are things I would like to take back
Sorry for not loving you right
I hope to make it up with dinner and candle lights
I never want to see you cry
I never want to wipe tears from your eyes

I never want to say sorry again,
Especially to my very best friend.

Sorry, sorry, sorry
For taking your love for granted

So sorry, sorry, sorry,
For taking your love for granted,
It was because I did not understand it.

Her Lion

You're the king of my jungle,
Yes that's what you are.
With you in my jungle
I know we'll go far

You talk with a powerful roar
How you do it, makes me feel secure

Your strength and drive,
Will keep us alive.
Your mane is a wonderful beauty
And to provide with love will be your duty

So your family will not lack
You must constantly be on the attack

For food which we will call prey
Which you must provide every day

Because you are the king of my jungle
A strong lion you are

Roar, Roar, Roar!!!

Minding My Own Business

Minding my own business one fine day
Walking in the park with nothing to say

Then ran a little puppy who clung to me
Then a scream from the park,
"That's my puppy!"
Then what crossed my eyes
Was a fine, beautiful pie.

Beautiful eyes that mesmerize
A great figure and soft to the touch
She has too much
That day I knew I had to take this chance
To find romance

It just happened to be, her pup clung to me
We became best friends that day in the month of May
She was right by my side,
And soon became my beautiful bride.

The Vow I Made

"I take you to be my (wife)
To have and to hold from this day forward
For better or for worse
For richer, for poorer, in sickness and in health
To love and to cherish
Till death do us part
According to God's Holy Law
And this is my solemn vow!"
Was every word you said true?
Was it from the heart?
What will happen when he or she gets you mad,
Or makes you sad?
Please remember your vow?
What would happen when the bills are not paid?
Remember the vow?
What would happen in the time of illness,
And the money isn't there?
What would you do?
Please, remember your vow but always
Pray and God the Father will find a way

The Crush I Had On You

When we were young
And did not have much sense
I said I like you.
Was this love?
Twenty years later I am
Still defending and providing
is this love?
The crush happened many years ago,
But I know it's love
Now I know emphatically, 'It was love!'

My College Wonder

I met her in college
On her quest for knowledge
You had a mind and great intellect
And lover of knowledge
And a student who looks real fine
I do not know what, but she is mine
Somehow this college intellect,
I earned her respect
I made her laugh every single day
It was hard for us to stay away
Sometimes I still wonder what she saw in me
But I must admit
we are a great fit
And hope to grow stronger, day by day, I love you

Love Me

Love me with your mind
Love me with your soul
Love me with your body
Love me with the tangible thing
Love me in the morning
Love me in the evening

Love me
Love me when I am difficult
Love me when I am sad
Love me when I am happy
Love me

Love me when I am hurting
Love me when I'm in pain
Love me when I am laughing
Love me
Love me all ways
Love me
Love me in times of plenty
Love me in times of poverty
Love me
Love me all ways
Love me

Matthew 19:5,6

4. And he answered and said unto them
Have ye not read that he
Which made them at the beginning
Made them male and female

5. And said, for this cause shall a man
Leave father and mother and
Shall cleave to his wife: and they
Twain shall be one flesh?

6. Wherefore they are no more
Twain, but one flesh
What therefore, God hath joined
Together. Let not man put asunder
Ephesians: 5:25

Husbands, love your wives, even as Christ,
also loved the church
And gave himself for it

Treat Her Like A Lady (And She Will)

Treat her like a lady
And she will love you

Treat her like a lady
And you will be the better for it

Treat her like a lady
She will give you her all

Treat her like a lady
She will never let you fall

Treat her like a lady
And you will know her mind and soul
Treat her like a lady
And you will earn her respect

Treat her like a lady
And be there to protect

Treat her like a lady
And she will give you her hand in marriage

Treat her like a lady
And she will make you the happiest man in the world

Treat her like a lady
And only death do us part
So, treat her like a lady

Please, Do Not Tell Me, "No"

May I have your hands in marriage?
And please do not tell me, No
May I have your hands in marriage?
And my love for you will show
May I have your hands in marriage?
My life I vow to live
May I have your hands in marriage?
You will make me the happiest man in the world
May I have your hands in marriage?
You will be my great pearl
May I have your hand in marriage
And please do not tell me, No!

The Pain Of A Broken Heart
(I Thought)

I thought your love would last forever,
But it did not
I thought our hearts would be one
But it wasn't meant to be
I thought you said you will never leave me
But you did
I thought we would grow old together
But you left me
I thought this pain would go away
But it still hurts
I thought the memories would fade
But you are still on my mind
It's the pain of a broken heart
You left me
The pain of a broken heart

Lovers Leap

Meeting you for the first time
My heart leaped
Looking into your eyes
And knowing I had your attention
My heart leaped

You asked the first question
That I had no answer to
Yet my heart leaped
Little did I know
I had the same affect on you
My heart leaped

You are in my thoughts and dreams
And I can't get you out of my mind
My heart still leaps

With this ring
And the song I will sing
I'm asking your hand in marriage
I know my heart will leap
With extra beats
Because you have my heart
Lover's leap
In to the unknown
Because you make my heart leap with extra beats

-Harold Johnson

Father To Son

My son, the road to finding love may cause you pain,
But if done right, you will gain
A lover, a wife and a very good friend and the relationship
will never end.
Son, when you find this precious gem treat her like a lady

Your life will be grand
Because you would have understood, what love is
So, love her, respect her and care for her
And treat her like a lady
From father to son

Part Time Lover

I don't think you're cheating
But our hearts are not meeting
Are we part-time lovers?

And even though you're here
I feel like you don't care
Are we part time lovers?
I need your full attention
And full devotion
Or are you a part time lover?

My heart is at stake
And I don't need a mistake
Or my love for granted to take
Are you a part time lover?

Let's call it quits
And do the split
Because our hearts are not in it
Part-time lover

Please don't do me wrong
While my feeling for you is so strong
I do not want to be a part-time lover

The Tears She Cried

The tears she cried
Because she was hurting
Deep inside

Rejected because you found another
And did not bother to let her know
She found out through a friend
That the relationship was at the end

The tears you cried
You pretend that our love it strong
For that you are wrong
A genuine heart you left wounded
Why? It still hurts inside

The tears she cried
With time this heart will be mended
And may find love again
But hopefully with a true good friend

The Author's Thought On Love

Here is something to keep in mind
when love you seek to find

Character
The mental and moral qualities of the person

Personality
The habitual behaviors or cognitions
and emotional patterns

Physicality
The fact of relating to the body as opposed to the
mind physical presence

Spirituality
The quality of being concerned with the human spirit or such
as opposed the material or physical

If these things are in place, your time you will not waste

So cautiously proceed
For there is no need for speed
Read the signs well
Use your own pace
Enjoy the chase
And complete the race
By finding true love

Clay In The Hands Of A Sculptor

My love for you is like
Clay in the hands of a sculptor
You work with precision
In a beautiful way
You shape and mould me
Like a beautiful piece of act
For it's you who have my heart
You handle me with grace and charm
In your hands I won't be alarmed
I am like clay in the hands of a sculptor
I know when you are done
I will be a master piece
A beauty to behold
And more precious than gold
Your master piece

My Busy Bee

You are like a busy bee
Working for me
Every plant, flower or tree
You go looking for honey for me

You prepare in the summer
When there is much to eat
And when winter and spring do appear
We will still have much to spare
My busy bee

I know you love me
For the work do show
How much you love me
I will never know
My busy bee

Keep up the work
My busy bee
And a happy family
We will be

An Angel In Disguise

You must have come from above
An angel in disguise
That's what you are

Your kindness and tender care
And for all the times you were there
To help, guide and provide for me
You cause me to see
That God has sent you to me
My angel in disguise

The words you say soothes the heart
And brings comfort to the soul
You are my angel in disguise

I never see you angry or in despair
I know that there is something there
You are an angel in disguise

I thank God for sending
You into my life
You're my angel in disguise

Just The Two of Us

In a world where there are
Millions of people
How did our heart meet
And fall for each other
Just the two of us

I can't see myself with anyone else
But you and I know you feel the same way too
Just the two of us

We love doing things together
And basking in each other's embrace
Be holding each other's face
Just the two of us

In my heart this is forever
I will not seek another
If just the two of us

May God bless your love
Just the two of us

We're Going All The Way

I tell you that I do
And these words are still true
We're going all the way

When I got down on my knees
And ask for your hand in marriage
I pledge with an oath to love you
So we're going all the way

The vow I made was sealed in heaven
And God, the Father was our witness
Know that they are still true
We're going all the way

Honey I love you
And we're going all the way

Her Lips

Soft and kissable is her lips
When she speaks, it's like perfume
Sweet smelling words, that bless

Her lips guide with wisdom
Soft and sweet

Her lips
Speak, love and compassion
She will give you her last
If need be

Her lips
Nurture, care and protect
Those she love and care for

Her kisses heal
Her kisses show compassion
Her kisses show love
Her kisses show me
Who I am
All this was from her lips

That's My Baby

As beautiful as can be and she is the one looking at me
That's my baby

Her mind is a beautiful thing
And she can also sing
That's my baby
I want to pledge my life, with this ring
That's my baby

I want to give her the key to my heart
So that our lives can truly start
That's my baby

We talk every night
When the moon is bright
With candle lights
That's my baby

The wind blows
Her fragrance fills the air
And it lingers there
That's my baby

I tell her often I love her
With heart, mind, and soul
For she is the only one I want to hold
That's my baby

-Tianna Johnson

A Singing Bird

It was a Wednesday morning
Day break was dawning

And in the trees the birds were singing
A melodious tune
It sounded so majestic
I had to take note of it

It was like, it was singing to me
It was sweet music to my ear

Then all of a sudden the sound that was so
Near it seems to have disappeared

It was that beautiful Wednesday morning
When I heard sweet music in my ear

A Walk to Remember

A road I often traveled, with lots of beautiful scenery
But it was this one sight that caught my eyes
and that was you
A beautiful sight to remember

She mesmerized me with her stunning beauty
Her eyes were a light shade of brown
Her lips were ruby red
This beautiful lady was a sight to remember

I happened to ask what's her name
And she obliged and from that day on
she became my best friend

So one year later, she became my wife
and brought joy to my life
What a beautiful walk to remember

-Tianna Johnson

Loving You Is Easy

Loving you is easy because you are beautiful

Loving you is easy because you are pleasing to the eyes

Loving you is easy because I earn your respect

Loving you I'll have it no other way

Loving you, it's forever
From loving you, I will stray never

Because loving you is easy
I love you

By The Sea

By the sea it was just you and me
Walking hand in hand

Leaving footprints in the sand
Just you and me

This feels so right
I can take this into the night
Just you and me

I was with a good friend
So I did not want it to end
Just you and me

It was a beautiful walk by the sea
Hand in hand leaving footprints
Just you and me

Shining Like A Diamond

Shining like a diamond is your love
A stunning beauty is your love

You are of great worth

Encased in pure gold
A beauty to behold
Is what you are

The intensity of your beauty is breathtaking

When I gaze into your heart
I get lost in your love

Keep shining keep mesmerizing
For that's what you are
A beautiful diamond

Her Teddy Bear

The one that is always there
The one who always stare
And its like it cares
Her teddy bear

I hug you at night
And you feel just right
My teddy bear

I want to wake up one day
And be happy to say
My teddy bear is here and he is near
And I love how he feel
My teddy bear

I will hold him forever
And let him go never
My teddy bear

A Four Letter Word

A four letter word that carries a lot of weight

It can stop you in your track
It can make you stop and take note
It can make the heart skip a beat
It can change your mind
And cause you to be on time.

It can make you spend a lot
Can put you on the spot.

It can spin your head
And make the eyes red
Yes it is love.

Love is the key to the heart
Love done right will not come apart.

A four letter word that carries lots of power.
It keep, it guides, it protect, its kind, its warm.

And it brings two hearts together
Yes it's love.
It's powerful, weighty and strong
Yes it's love.

This Is Forever

The vow I made to take your hand
And to be your man
Was and is forever

I was so serious with this thing
I went out and bought the beautiful ring

I swear not to have another
Because you are the one who have my heart
And as long as life last
You will be a great part

This love is forever
For it's you who have my heart.

I love you.

I Pray For You

I pray for you everyday
That God the father would
Be your stay
And that we will never stray

I pray for eyes only for you
Ears only to hear your voice

I pray that my lips would only kiss you and to speak
Loving words in your ear

I pray for hands that will make all your dreams come true
For feet that will run always to do your will
I pray for a steadfast devotion to only you

This is my prayer in Jesus' name,
Amen

Going Strong

When you caught my eyes
It was no surprise
We fell in love

And everyday that goes by
Our love grow stronger and stronger

You may ask, "Why?"

Because we put in the time
And effort to build this relationship
And put it on a firm foundation

There is still work to do
When words are put into action
To her it is a strong attraction

You say what you mean
And mean what you say
And it's put on display

So in the years to come
We will continue to build on
This strong foundation
With God's help

Beautiful As A Peach

One of the most beautiful fruit
To behold is a peach

It's beautiful two tone color
That blends so very well

The red and yellow
Each color stunning in it's own right
And vibrantly bright, my peach

This is my attempt to describe you:
You are so beautiful,
Just like a peach

Firm and sweet plump and round
A pleasure to enjoy,
That's my peach

How you treat me
You stole my heart
You are my beautiful peach

The Girl Has Game

She knew she was fine,
And she has a brilliant mind.

So she put her plan in motion
To capture his heart

The things she did to get
His attention was so easy:

A hail and a wink
And the boy could not think.
He lost his mind
Over the love he found

Her game was tight
And things turned out right.

The girl, got game!

She Is The Real Deal

My girl, she speaks her mind
For she is one of a kind

You will know how she feels
Because she keeps it real

She is the real deal

I love her very much
She has that special touch

Honey continue to speak your mind
And you will be just fine
For you are the real deal

And she has my heart

A Thousand Ways To Say I LOVE You

Tell me you love me in a thousand ways
And you can have my love.
I want to know that every word you say is true and real
And that what you say is truly felt.
I want to feel your every expression
And look into your eyes when each word is said.
The words "I love you" can only be used once.
And when this task begins, I know we'll have lot's of fun
With every rising of the sun.
The day and time is for your own choosing
And any strategy or method is for your using.
Poetry, words, rhythm, and rhyme
May be used at any time.
Please do not attempt this task in just one day
Because it's not a game that children play.
And I ask that you be real and sincere
For human hearts need special care.
Love is the ultimate task
And if done right, it will surely last.
So please have fun as you seek romance
For this is your greatest chance.

Constant Love

Love is like a big, old toy,
In the hands of a little boy.
Holding it very close to his chest,
Because it's special and it's the best.
When I reflect on our great love,
I must confess that you are from above.
When I whisper in your ear,
I tell you things you need to hear,
I hope that constantly you will know,
How much my love for you will grow.
"I love you."

I Am A Promise Keeper

I told her that I love her, and that is true,
But I know in my heart there is much work to do.
To keep the hope of this love alive,
I know that I must always strive
to do the very best I can
And try to understand
the things that will make her love me more,
And all of the joys God has in store.
For she is the one who has my heart,
and our love is set apart.
A commitment was made and it is clear to see,
that I am happy she has chosen me.
I will be faithful to every word I make,
And her love for granted, I will never take.
I will pour out my heart like a fountain,
and dare to climb the highest mountain,
to prove to her that this love I have for her is real,
And to show you exactly how I feel.
My dear, know one thing and that is this:
My love for you, you'll never miss,
Because I will be there by your side
And my devotion for you, I will not hide.
So I promise to love you with every move I make,
and with every breath I take,
And a happy home to make,
May God bless our love...

If I Could Love

If I could love, who would it be?
If I could love, would I be able to see?
If I could love, would it be real?
If I could love, what would I feel?
If I could love, would I get hurt?
If I could love, what would it be worth?
If I could love, would it bring me joy?
Or would I be used like a child's toy?
If I could love, would it touch my heart?
Would I lose the greater part?
If I could love, would I suffer loss?
Or would love pay the cost?
If I could love, how will I know?
Who will be the one to show?
If I could love, will it make me cry?
And will the same one be there to dry my teary eyes?
If I could love, when can I begin?
And in the end, will I win?

It's Time Again

It's that time again when flowers and chocolates
Become the order of the day.
And love is rekindled in a brand new way.
Great efforts to impress
And the way we will dress
Speak of the passion of the time.
The colours of choice are very bright,
And they are red and white.
A quiet dinner for two,
And the best choice wine.
Things are looking just fine.
You continue the evening way into the night
And it all worked out just right.

Like A Rose

My love for you is oh, so strong.
With you in my arms I can't go wrong.
You're like a rose showing its elegance
And somehow you draw me in with
The intensity of your stunning beauty.
You blossom like springtime in the air
And when you are ready, nothing can compare.
As each day goes by, you become "soft and sweet"
And with you, there is none that can compete.
Like the depth of the deepest ocean,
I will not hide my love and devotion.
My love for you grows deeper
With each passing day,
And I will never go astray.
I now bring this poem to a close,
You will always be my special rose.

Love, O' Love

Love, o'love, why do you treat me this way?
You trample my heart and then
have nothing to say.
You play with my emotions and you mess with my mind,
And you know that this love was specially designed!
The words I express, you know they are true,
For you know what I say, is always what I do.
Please tell me, "What more I can do,
To make this love last forever?"
The moon and the stars are not mine to give,
But a life for you, I vow to live.
Love, o'love, why do you treat me this way?
You trample my heart and then have nothing to say.

Love Target

Love is like an arrow,
Aiming straight to the heart
And once I've found my target
I will never depart.
I've found my love and that is you.
I always try to be true.
I hope we can start as the best of friends
So that our relationship will never end.
With every moment and breath I take,
My love for you, I'll never forsake.
I hope our years be bright as gold
So that we grow in grace when we get old.
Having more love than from the start,
When you placed your arrow in my heart.
If by chance, we must depart,
You will always be in my heart.
I Love You.

Marriage

Marriage is an honourable thing,
When two hearts are joined and wedding bells ring.
Devoting their lives to each other,
And swearing not to love another.
Living life in sweet accord,
And the fruit of the womb is their great reward.
Endeavouring to share in life's good and bad,
And to accept the sweet and the sad.
Marriage, has God ordained,
That the holy sanctity of marriage shall remain
Between this man and his wife,
And with God leading their lives.
If we be willing to be used by God.
Our precious marriage, He will reward.
With love and kindness as we grow,
And His guidance will forever show.

Roses Are Red,
Violets Are Blue

Roses are red, violets are blue,
And here is something special and true.
I behold something more precious than gold,
And my dear, that is you.
You impress me with your mind
And your great intellect,
And that is how you earned my respect.
Darling, your figure is so fine,
And I'm happy that you are mine.
I Love You.

Treasured Love

The love that is ours is more precious than
gold and diamonds
And there is nothing that can compare.
Rubies and jaspers could only describe some
of your qualities.
Diamonds describe your beautiful eyes
And the way that they mesmerize.
Gold speaks to your presence.
It radiates a strong beam of light,
That causes others to shine when around you.
Your mind and intellect can hold my attention.
Your beauty and figure I have no need to mention!
There are many things I could say,
That would express the way you make me feel.
But, honestly, "I love you," is the only way
that I can keep it real.

Wildflower

Looking at you reminds me of nature and its beauty.
I see a wildflower in full bloom
And know that something "wonderful is about to happen".
It's like spring is in the air, for your fragrance lingers there.
You light up my senses like the cold morning dew
To get my attention, that's what you do.
Thank you for the colour and joy
And happiness you bring to my life.
I love you.

Marriage
...and Then Some

Marriage
...and Then Some

Marriage is the beautiful union of two souls coming together in covenant, vowing to live a life of faithfulness, truth and loyalty to one another. This covenant holds through good times and bad times, rich times and poor times, and in sickness and health. What a covenant!

The more I think about the covenant of marriage, the more it blows me away. I see marriage in the Almighty God, who ordained marriage in the Garden of Eden.

The Bible tells us that while doing God's work in The Garden, Adam began to feel lonely. So, the Wise Creator stepped in and put Adam to sleep and removed one of his ribs. He fashioned the woman for the man "and oh, what a difference"! God brought the woman to the man, and Adam declared her, 'the bone of his bones and the flesh of his flesh.' Adam gave her the name, 'Ishshah (Woman). Then, God united them in covenant to each other.

Many of us know of people who have been married for decades, some twenty, thirty or even sixty years and it is clear that those who are lasting, took their marriage vows

very seriously. Certainly, these couples faced many troubles
and pain, but they also experienced laughter and joy with
each other. God then blessed their marriage by allowing
them to love each other and by providing for their needs.
Today, the word marriage seems to have taken on a whole
new meaning and the vows a couple make to each other
seem to be ingenuine. Many have disregarded the purpose
for marriage and cave in to the desires for money or even the
pressure to get married from family members and friends.
While a few of these marriages do last, most of these couples
do not even make it to their second or third wedding anni-
versary.
Based on my observations, many marriages do not last for
several other reasons. We will now discuss these in detail.

Time

Time is one of the most important elements of a relation-
ship. Time heals, time brings forth growth, and time draws
us closer to each other and brings depth to our relationships.
The Bible speaks about time in Ecclesiastes 3.
*1 There is a time for everything, and a season for every ac-
tivity under heaven: 2 a time to be born and a time to die, a
time to plant and a time to uproot, 3 a time to kill and a time
to heal, a time to tear down and a time to build, 4 a time to
weep and a time to laugh, a time to mourn and a to dance,
5 a time to scatter stones and a time to gather them, a time to
embrace and a time to refrain, 6 a time to search and a time
to give up, a time to keep and a time to throw away, 7 a time
to tear and a time to mend, a time to be silent and a time to
speak, 8 a time to love and a time to hate, a time for war and
a time for peace..."*
The Bible puts even more importance on time and the usage
of it. Using your time wisely in your relationships is very
important. We should be extremely cautious about what we
say and ensure that it is the right time to do so. A vital part
of communication involves taking the time to listen to what
your mate feels and why.
Additionally, there is 'a time to simplify your life'. Take
a look at your weekly schedule. Perhaps it may be wise to
eliminate certain activities that are consuming time that
needs to be spent ministering to your loved ones.

Habits And Behaviour

Again, the essence of time comes into play. One must know the person they are getting involved with. Consider whether or not you can really live with this person for the rest of your life, before you make a major commitment to get married. Be sure to take your time and really observe their habits. There is no need to rush.

While there are both bad and good habits, we must realize that they will not show immediately. The appearance of love often causes us to only see the good in people and completely ignore their faults that we also need to be paying attention to. Habits and behaviours will always be apart of the human make up and that's the way it will always be.

Compatibility

As a couple, you should also be sure that you enjoy doing things together and that you enjoy each other's company. This makes a strong relationship. Many relationships end because the couples weren't really compatible with each other. The couple simply could not 'see eye to eye.' Remember that just because two persons are physically attracted to each other, does not make them compatible.

Faith

If you are a Christian, be sure that you are not unequally yoked with your significant other. This is a very touchy topic and I see it happen around me very frequently and often times, neither husband nor wife were a Christian at the time of the marriage. Day-in and day-out, one must pray for the salvation of his/her spouse. Otherwise, the non-Christian spouse can become a stumbling block for the Christian. In this scenario, the Christian must also pray fervently and ask God for wisdom, patience and strength. Be sure that you do not impose your faith on your spouse. He/she should have a desire to join you in your rebirth just by seeing the way you live.

Baggage

In this day and age, many individuals go through several relationships before they find the right one. This can bring non-idealistic baggage into any new relationship. This can happen for several reasons and may be in the form of a child or children, hurts from past relationships, divorces, the illness or death of a loved one, and even low self esteem. If you are in a relationship with someone who may be carrying a lot of baggage, handle them with care. You do not want your marriage to fail. While it is not ideal for persons to come into a marriage with baggage, the truth is that it happens. Do all that you can to lighten the load and to avoid carrying baggage into a marriage, be careful about who you let into your life and who you pursue a relationship with.

Money Management

Improper money management is a problem that has existed among couples for ages. I have seen this one problem cause so many marriages and families to break up. Between paychecks being spent at web shops, trying to 'keep up with Joneses' and living above your means, and several other addictions, the essential needs to sustain a home are often overlooked. Many times, spouses keep separate bank accounts that the other person does not even know of.
This can be avoided by being disciplined in the way that finances are kept. Always consult your spouse before spending and set weekly budgets. Work together to accomplish household goals.

Abuse

Abuse is a huge threat to the sustainability of today's family. When a member of a family is being abused, both physical and mental scars are left that sometimes never go away. I am so perturbed by the way that a man can put his hands on a woman he claims to love, then make love to her afterwards. Even women abusing their husbands is becoming more and more popular nowadays.

Some men abuse their spouse because they believe it is the way to establish control in their relationship. Additionally, some men see the woman as a possession, or 'something' to conquer.

Some people also suffer emotional abuse that often leaves scars that are deeper than those left by physical abuse. The effects of this are often passed on to children. God placed a very complexed, yet delicate and fragile emotional structure in us. Harmful words will eat at us and tear us down. This is why I disagree with the popular idiom, 'Sticks and stones may break my bones, but words can never harm me.' Words can leave scars so deep that counselling is often needed to begin healing. This is why so many people are bitter, overly defensive and sometimes even evil.

Trust

Trust is a another important element in any relationship. To me, trust is the faithful certainty of the character and the morality of the one you swear to love. You should have total confidence in your spouse without having any doubts in your mind about his/her character. Unfortunately, many husbands and wives cannot feel this way. Many times, infidelity is the main reason for distrust in the relationship. Other reasons include wandering eyes, not spending enough time at home or with your spouse and withholding sex from your spouse. Many homes are destroyed because of distrust in the marriage and often times, once your partner breaks your trust, it's very hard to gain it back. A rebuilding process can begin however, once your partner is ready to confess their mistake and be committed to regaining your trust. Remember to be willing to forgive as Christ has forgiven you.
In conclusion, I urge you to treat your spouse with the most respect. If you are not married yet, be wise about your selection and remember that your wedding vows are a covenant with God. Take them seriously!

Notes